Crucifixion of GCAC Alliance Church by C&MA
Copyrighted (2014) – Ven G. Cheock
ISBN: 978-0-578-14128-2

TABLE OF CONTENTS

Description

This book narrates a tragedy at the Grace Community Alliance Church (GCAC) congregation in Baldwin Park, California where the "shepherds" – namely: the Christian & Missionary Alliance National Office (referred to as C&MA - http://www.cmalliance.org) and the C&MA South Pacific District (SPD) Superintendent (http://www.cmalliance.org/district/south-pacific) – facilitated the conditions and under the pretext of the "reversionary clause" systematically preyed on the flock they are supposed to be guarding and nurturing. GCAC is one of the several C&MA congregations where these "shepherds" seized the assets without the consent of the congregation who paid for the property since inception, and the "shepherds" during the course of perpetrating the "crucifixion" of GCAC have employed manipulative, corrupt and other inappropriate tactics reminiscent of oppressors in banana republics, and unworthy of institutions claiming to be the "shepherds" and "guardians" of the church.

Why write this book?

The C&MA stakeholders and the public should know the tragedy at GCAC and other C&MA congregations, and I hope that this will serve as a deterrent in other congregations falling victim to predators in sheep's clothing - within and outside of C&MA.

I am not a writer but my passion in distinguishing between right and wrong and the capacity to plead a case, far supersede those who call themselves as the "shepherds" and "guardians" of the church, an institution that has clearly lost its way.

Who crucified Jesus Christ?

There were the high priest, the priests, the rulers and the elders of the Jewish people, the scribes, Pharisees and Sadducees. The Romans also had a large part in the Crucifixion: Pilate, the governor of the Roman providence, gave the order and his soldiers carried it out.

Who crucified the GCAC Congregation?

There were the Christian & Missionary Alliance National Office (C&MA - http://www.cmalliance.org) National Office and C&MA South Pacific District (SPD) Superintendent (http://www.cmalliance.org/district/south-pacific). In tandem, these 2 groups crucified GCAC (and other C&MA congregations), efficiently performing the equivalent functions of the high priest, the priests, the rulers, the elders of the Jewish people, the scribes, Pharisees and Sadducees and the Romans.

Who coveted the property of GCAC?

There were the Christian & Missionary Alliance National Office (C&MA - http://www.cmalliance.org) and C&MA South Pacific District (SPD) Superintendent (http://www.cmalliance.org/district/south-pacific).
When the congregation purchased the GCAC in Baldwin Park in 1983, it was worth a lot less than the $1.3 million that was sold for (please refer to Attachment A).

Summary

1) Attachment A – GCAC For Sale Advertisement
2) Attachment B - Email to AFC President Bong and Pastor Felix Ballon, April 8, 2014. Last letter to AFC Filipino Alliance Pastors asking questions. Does GCAC has to die?
3) Attachment C – The Demise of GCAC Alliance Church, April 4, 2014. My letter to all C&MA Alliance Pastors in South Pacific District Area and Alliance Lay leaders regarding closure and padlocking of GCAC church.
4) Attachment D – Email for AFC President Pastor Bong, March 25, 2014. About "Money" and "suffered the brother's demise to win another brother souls?" is this OK?
5) Attachment E – Email to Pastor Bong, March 21, 2014. My answers to Pastor Bong's five allegations. "No GCAC Congregational Meeting at all." C&MA, SPD and AFC LEADERSHIP did ecclesiastical immorality and God Words are very clear. The IRRESPONSIBLE SHEPHERDS?
6) Attachment F – Email to Our Brothers Mission with Thanks, March 14, 2014. My first reaction, No C&MA pastor license, free indeed!
7) Attachment G – Email to Pastor Bong, March 14, 2014. AFC president defending C&MA SPD Superintendent.

8) Attachment H – Email: Our Brothers Mission with Thanks, March 13, 2014. Last letter to GCAC church leadership. The C&MA decision and actions are final and binding.
9) Attachment I – Final Appeal Letter to Dr. John Stumbo, November 8, 2013. The last resort, our final Appeal to C&MA Alliance National Office to cease the sale of GCAC property.
10) Attachment J – GCAC Brief History, April 16, 2014

Next steps

This book will be updated every two years and will document our next steps. I could be reached at vgcheock@yahoo.com.

Attachment A – GCAC for Sale Advertisement

PROPERTY HIGHLIGHTS

- Approximately 6,524 SF Church property
- Lot size approximately 1.20 acres
- Sanctuary seats approximately 175
- ±65 parking spaces
- Fellowship hall, kitchen
- Offices, classrooms and storage rooms
- Large Fenced Outdoor Area
- **Asking Price $1,395,000**

For more information, please contact:

ERIC KNOWLES	ROBERT FLETCHER	JIMMY CHAI	CUSHMAN & WAKEFIELD OF SAN DIEGO, INC.
Senior Director	Associate Director	Associate Director	Lic. #01329963
(213) 955-5132 | (858) 558-5617	(213) 955-5133 | (858) 558-5618	(213) 955-5134	4747 Executive Drive, 9th Floor
eric.knowles@cushwake.com	robert.fletcher@cushwake.com	jimmy.chaai@cushwake.com	San Diego, CA 92121
Lic. #00944210	Lic. #01706060	Lic. #01806325	www.cushmanwakefield.com

Attachment B - Email to AFC President Bong and Pastor Felix Ballon, April 8, 2014

From: Ven Cheock

April 8, 2014

To AFC President Bong and Pastor Felix Ballon,
Cc: All FILIPINO Alliance Pastors and Church Leaders,
Cc: C&MA National Office, C&MA SPD, CAMACOP

My personal greetings to you in the name of Jesus Christ, our Lord!

I know that you have a scheduled AFC Pastor Conference in Sacramento, CA. on April 21. I was verbally invited by two pastors to attend being an Elder of previous GCAC Filipino Church.

AFC Filipino churches former FACAMA:

Let me state that "AFC birth mother was GCAC CHURCH".
Founder Elder Fred Pamaran, Pastor Apelar and Pastor Hernan Pada were the elder fathers. First president was Pastor H. Pada.

With all honesty, I have several questions to you regarding the demise of GCAC. Before my questions, let me qualify my standing positions.
I did consult my Counselor Alliance Pastors in all my actions.

My standing with my Brother, Pastor Fred Cheock:

I am an Elder of GCAC church with him. Naturally, we have administrative differences. We are not perfect leaders, infallible, therefore I left, temporarily separated from GCAC in 2004.

My standing with GCAC church:

I love GCAC church. I was with the church since 1978-2004 (26 years), I served, enjoyed, I loved the church body loving fellowship. I left with my plan to return at a later time. I consider myself a remnant GCAC member, I worship and fellowship with another church but I am not a member of any, because I will return to GCAC.

In June 2012, I came to know my brother was removed by the SPD SUPERINTENDENT. Rightfully or otherwise, my advice to him was to submit, because he was under a superior SPD superintendent. I pleaded for GCAC restoration.

With counsel, I wrote a letter to CMA SPD inquiring about GCAC membership. In 2012, SPD, AS Rev. Steve Riley replied that GCAC church will be closed by DEXCOM (9/14/12, email). I continued pleading, begging to C&MA for "GCAC RESTORATION". They all fell into deaf ears.

With AFC president Bong and Pastor Felix Ballon:

Yes! You two intervened at the request of the SPD superintendent with sweet talk of "$$$$" (email). Isn't that a shame? A lure of "Money"? Have you contributed any amount during 28 years at the GCAC property? So, you are mercenaries? The responsibility of the superintendent was given to you? You claimed all Filipino pastors were in agreement? (By your email). In another email, SPD claimed all AFC pastors approved too? Isn't this statement a lie? Where is the proof? Don't you need to explain to all our Filipino Alliance Pastors? And to the C&MA leadership?

You claimed you are the Constituted Authority? By C&MA constitutional authority to your own church? Yes! Does it extend to another church? Who instigated to the Demise of GCAC church? Aren't you, are familiar with killing of Jesus? The High Priests instigated Roman Governor to crucify Jesus?

You are licensed to C&MA AUTHORITY:

With encumbered position can you not express your divergent opinion? With fear? Hook, line and sinker you have followed? Even in unrighteousness? Particularly when Money "$$$" is involved?

Does the failure of the church's Pastor enough reason to close, dissolve, sell the church property?
Does the failure of Church leader's reason to padlock the church? Scatter the congregation?

Does GCAC and Paramount Alliance Churches need to die for preaching the gospel to multiply more churches? To the Filipino ministry? By the Christian and Missionary Alliance, Superintendent, SPD, DEXCOM?

God forbid!

Truly I grieved greatly for the many precious souls who left and were scattered.

Truly I grieved for the loss of GCAC loving fellowships of the brethren.

Truly I grieved for the vibrant GCAC ministry for 32 fruitful years.

What killed them? Sin? Greed? "Money"? Fraud? Lies? Legal constituted authority?
"Carnality?"

May the good Lord, our Great God, Jesus Christ be the judge!

My recommendation conclusion:

We are "Filipino" congregation. Our ethnic sensitivity as loving people is different. While in America, as Christians, an Oversea Filipinos, we still carry our "Filipino" loving way. Our fellowship lunch is true hospitality and brotherhood. Brotherhood is true Christian way. I still wish and dream the revival of GCAC loving fellowship. I carry "No" bitterness, just brotherhood to all.

Last question, Can AFC be a "Filipino District?

May God grant us His PEACE!

Brother Ven Cheock

Attachment C – The Demise of GCAC Alliance Church, April 4, 2014

From: Ven Cheock

April 4, 2014.

To all Alliance Pastors and Lay Leaders:

Greetings in the name of Jesus.

As an Elder of the GCAC Church, I sadly share the tragic demise of the church and the suffering of its members under the District superintendents of the C&MA, South Pacific District (SPD) in Los Angeles, CA.

Between 2004 and 2012, due to pastor doctrinal difference and member issues, the members split from the congregation and the church elders/leadership wrote complaint letters to the superintendent. During these seven years, the superintendent did nothing to address the issues. When the SPD district finally came in, the Superintendent dissolved the congregation without consent. With the inept handling of the situation, the congregation languished and scattered like the broken glasses. While a handful of members remained, the church was classified to a "redevelopment" status. The church's demise followed shortly after year 2012.

In 2012, we received a letter from the superintendent removing the pastor due to an administrative issue. The new superintendent, DS Rev. Malick made a radical move of padlocking the church. The church was reopened by the church leaders. Then, without congregational approval or consent, the superintendent took over, closed the church, dissolved the congregation, transferred the church property to the District, and re-padlocked the church property until it was sold in about January 2014. Since 2012, the members appealed for GCAC restoration in many letters but were ignored.

Appeal history:

The GCAC congregation leadership appealed to the C&MA national office in late 2013, then in March, 2014. The C&MA National Office replied in a letter said that the action made by the SPD is final and binding.

Plead history:

For ten (10) long years, we pleaded for assistance from the CMA superintendents, and for the recent two (2) years since 2012, we pleaded for restoration – all fell into deaf ears.

Twice in ten years, the administrative replies resulted in splitting the congregation rather than address and rule on the issue presented. With the scattering of the congregation, the church lost many members. While continuing our appeal for restoration, the CMA Superintendent applied the "REVERSIONARY" clause, sold the church property. For the record, since 1992, the church property was paid for 28 years by the GCAC Filipino congregation.

We had a strong GCAC Alliance Church of 100-200 members during the 32 memorable and endearing years. However, due to the problems documented in this letter, between 2004 and 2012, ninety-nine percent (99%) of the members left the church. The greatest losses are: grieved the loss of worship, loving fellowship of brothers and sisters in Christ, memories of children friendships, brotherhood, birthdays and marriages and many more memories; we scattered; some even lost the love of Christ due to questionable practices by the SPD and C&MA National Office.

The following anomalies were practiced by the C&MA, South Pacific District:

 1. Ignored the real issues, and classified the church into "redevelopment" status.
 2. Ignored the church members; 99% of the original members left.
 3. Cancelled congregational meeting for old and remaining members.
 4. Rallied support from encountered FILIPINO pastors and AFC president.
 5. Induced out interim pastor and congregation who sympathized GCAC case.
 6. Forced out remaining congregation, forced padlocked the church.
 7. The Superintendent took over the church leadership as president.
 8. Applied the CMA vs Alliance Church "REVERSIONARY" clause
 9. Quietly transferred the church property into itself (SPD) entity by the superintendent, now president
10. Dissolved the church California incorporation without making provisions for church members where to go.
11. Sweet talked the AFC Filipino pastors for "$$$" sharing.
12. Finally, Sold the church property early 2014.

CONCLUSION:

This is an alert letter regarding the REVERSIONARY Clause. It is a financial trap. The C&MA made use the "REVERSIONARY CLAUSE" in taking over the GCAC Church assets and other questionable practices in closing a church, by the C&MA, South Pacific District. I am hoping that this letter will educate and hinder other possible Alliance Church victims and deter such practices in the future.

By Ven Cheock

Email: vgcheock@yahoo.com

GCAC History:

From 1972 to 2004, a period of 32 years, the GCAC congregation and pastors enjoyed the affiliation with the C&MA, SPD Superintendents. The membership of the congregation increased. The Church Pastor Andy Apelar was honored as C&MA church planter. Pastor Hernan Pada planted the Paramount Alliance Church, a daughter church. Fully paid. Other new churches were formed in cities like San Diego. Missions included bible students with financial support in the Philippines for many years. Filipino Alliance Churches conducted joint services during Sunrise Service.

The year 2004 marked a turn of events. With pastor issues, the healthy church congregation was negatively affected by the mishandling of Superintendent, DS Rev. Don Burst. Over 60% of the congregation left, members scattered around the city. Humbly, the church leadership prayed that they would come back when the pastor was removed. However, the exodus of members continued and complaints increased.

By mid-2012, the Pastor was removed. Without congregational meeting and approval, the church was taken over by the superintendent, DS Rev. Malick. Then the church was padlocked. But the congregation reopened the church. I with the previous GCAC leadership repeatedly appealed for church restoration but were ignored. The SPD, district re-padlocked again and finally sold the GCAC property for sale in January, 2014, without congregation consent, this spelled the demise of GCAC Alliance Church.

More ....the REVERSIONARY clause!

"REVERSIONARY" clause:

This clause was used an excuse for the takeover. "REVERSIONARY" clause was intended to protect the congregation against greedy leadership. But this was used fraudulently and unjustly by the C&MA, District Leadership against the GCAC congregation. It was for financial gain for the million "$$$" property.

References are attached. If you need further proof and documents, please call me at 818 718-7552 or email me.

REFERENCE #1,

Other "Alliance Churches" Closed and Reverted:

1) CHRISTIAN & MISSIONARY ALLIANCE NAMED IN CONSPIRACY LAWSUIT FILED: CONSPIRACY TO DEFRAUD CHINESE CHURCH OF $650,000 CHURCH PROPERTY AND APPROXIMATELY $18,000 IN BANK ACCOUNTS by James Sundquist

2) Crestwood Alliance Church in Big Bend, St. Louis, Missouri, property worth $600,000, Leadership was sweet talked and closed, sold, Church congregation were scattered.

3) Community Church Of Paramus Of The Christian And Missionary Alliance, Community Church Of Paramus, Alliance church in Paramus, New Jersey, property fully paid was closed, reverted to C&MA.

4) Paramount Alliance Church in Paramount, CA, property worth million "$$$" was closed and reverted, now owned, rented by the C&MA, SPD DISTRICT.

REFERENCE #2,

A.
http://www.wnd.com/2012/07/church-occupied-after-offices-ransacked/

"A church building in California has been occupied by its elders after they found the offices ransacked, records and checkbooks gone and new locks on the building, all done by their own church conference in its process of "taking possession" of the structure and "securing the building," members have told WND.

The district leadership of the conference is pursuing a reversion clause that it says applies to conference churches, and official's most likely want to sell the church assets of some $1 million, even though the congregation and the pastor are pleading for mercy."................end of excerpt.

B.
http://witnessed.wordpress.com/2008/05/13/christian-missionary-alliance/

"CHRISTIAN & MISSIONARY ALLIANCE NAMED IN CONSPIRACY LAWSUIT FILED: CONSPIRACY TO DEFRAUD CHINESE CHURCH OF $650,000 CHURCH PROPERTY AND APPROXIMATELY $18,000 IN BANK ACCOUNTS by James Sundquist

In a major lawsuit, the Mid America District of the Christian & Missionary Alliance (hereafter C&MA) was named by a group of former members of the Chinese Alliance Church of Colorado Springs. The C&MA is one of the largest Evangelical Protestant Christian denominations, with 2,010 C&MA churches in the U.S., and 440 in Canada, with approximately 417,000 members in the United States. The Plaintiff has alleged that the C&MA conspired to defraud and subsequently confiscate and convert their $650,000 church property and assets and emptied their approximately $18,000 in bank accounts, located in Colorado Springs, Colorado, U.S.A. The Defendant, C&MA Mid America District Headquarters office, is located in Omaha, Nebraska. C&MA National Church Ministries Vice President Rev. John Soper endorsed and approved both the closure and the sale of the church property in two letters.....end of excerpt.

C.
Pastor H. Pada, as GCAC church assigned interim pastor was induced to leave with monetary consideration.

On Aug 3, 2012, Pastor Fred wrote: (excerpts).

Dear Ven, ... In Dec. 2010, superintendent, Rev. Bill Malik, closed the Paramount Alliance Church. In the midst of well qualified Paramount members' number, owned the church property with $40,000 in the bank, he

padlocked the church property with the intention to sell. After the meeting with the members of the Paramount, knowing the case, I asked the GCAC church board the authority to intervene.
In our [my] intervention, Rev. Malik decided not to sell the Paramount Church property...... Excerpt #1

[With GCAC], Rev. Bill Malick intentionally endeavored forcefully to financially break the church to place the church in redevelopment. Proof: Forcing Pastor Pada to move out, Rev. Bill Malick was giving $1,000 a month to force him to move out. ..... Excerpt # 2.

....
End of excerpts.......

REFERENCE #3,

Final Appeal Letter: to C&MA, national office. Complete copy.
Please refer to Attachment I – Final Appeal Letter to Dr. John Stumbo, November 8, 2013

Attachment D – Email for AFC President Pastor Bong, March 25, 2014

From: Ven Cheock

March 25, 2014

Dear pastor Bong,

In the previous email, I did answered with the truths of the 5 points you wrote.

Here is the 6 point,

You said "I have met with Rev. Bill Malick last week and he assured me that the money derived from the sale of the church building will be used for the growth and development of Filipino ministry in the Southern California area. .... Nothing is definite yet as we are still in the exploration stage. "......

My answer to you,

Money! "For the love of money is a root of all kinds of evil. Some people, eager for money, have wandered from the faith and pierced themselves with many grieves."

The bible said those words above.

Material gain with greed is like the bible picture story.

23 "When the soldiers crucified Jesus, they took his clothes, dividing them into four shares, one for each of them, with the undergarment remaining. This garment was seamless, woven in one piece from top to bottom.

24 "Let's not tear it," they said to one another. "Let's decide by lot who will get it."

This happened that the scripture might be fulfilled that said,

"They divided my clothes among them
    And cast lots for my garment."[a]
So this is what the soldiers did." End quote.

....

Sweet-Talk, to coax with sweet persuasion has many stories. You may want to find out what happened to the Crestwood Alliance Church in St. Louis, Missouri. It was sweet-talked, now it's gone, the members were scattered. I attended the church for 3 years in 1993-95.

AS, Pastor Steve Riley was the former pastor of the church until he came to SPD.

Another, "Natural Wild Animal Kingdom is God's design" is another story. Animal fights for the large Lion big catch such like a deer. Even scavengers' hyena, vulture, wild dogs, flock together for the share. They fight for survival. This animal behavior.

Jesus gospel is to win souls for his kingdom with love.
Isn't Jesus said, "Seek first the Kingdom of God and his Righteousness"
Please check the "Qualifications for Overseers and Deacons" in 1 Timothy.

Is "To seek Money first and suffered brother demise to win another brother souls" Ok?

May God, our Lord Jesus be the judge.

Only God be exalted.

Your brother in Christ.

Ven

Attachment E – Email to Pastor Bong, March 21, 2014

From: Ven Cheock

March 21, 2014

Dear Pastor Bong and greetings to all concerns.

In reply further to your letter as of March 14, 2014, I will dwell only in morality and theological aspect in my answers, not on the legal aspect.

The current issue is GCAC, CHURCH, it was unjustly closed (killed), padlocked, property sold, in Million of Dollar, by C&MA, SPD district with AFC pastor participation to Indonesian Buyer.

Below is your email claims and my answers,

1, You claimed, "As you know, I am an Official Licensed Worker of the Alliance and I take pride and guard my license very zealously because of what it stands............. I stand to put my name on the line in the defense of this great denomination and its leadership "....
You further claimed, "In as much as there is in our bylaws the "reversionary clause," we also have a stipulation on "constituted authority." What this means is that we as pastors made a covenant during our licensing interview as well as ordination interview to submit to the authority over us which is the District Leadership and the National Leadership. ....".end quote

2, You claimed, "The Association of Filipino Churches of the C&MA of which I am the president was asked to intervene. I rallied the other pastors in the area and with one voice, we supported the decision of the District to bring a change into the church "...end quote

My answer:

In short, you as AFC PRESIDENT, had participated in the demise of the church, GCAC, the Grace Community Alliance Church body of Christ, of which C&MA of South Pacific District unjustly killed (closed and dissolved) it.

Then, force padlocked, sold the asset and property for a million Dollar, WILL share the lion share $$$ among you. This is your term "Constituted Authority ".

Now! I have the Bible story, this refers to the two Constituted Authority together they killed our Lord, Jesus Christ ". Quoting the Bible,

"Governor Pilate tried to release him. But the Jewish leaders shouted out, everyone who claims to be a king opposes Caesar!" When Pilate heard these words he brought Jesus outside and Pilate said to the Jewish leaders, "Look, here is your king!"
Then they shouted out, "Away with him! Away with him! Crucify him!" Pilate asked, "Shall I crucify your king?" The high priests replied, "We have no king except Caesar!" Then Pilate handed him over to them to be crucified. Ref: John 19:12-16.

You see the Metaphor? Allegory?

The GCAC church was killed by C&MA, SPD, and AFC LEADERSHIP, by the two "Constituted Authority " both conspired together in killing Jesus Christ Church, Pastor Felix Ballon and You are part of the "Constituted Authority ".

....Note explain "Seek first the kingdom of God and his righteousness" vs. " Constituted Authority"

Pastor Bong, in going further,

3, You claimed that "The most logical step therefore is to padlock the church by the District and the AFC pastors are all in agreement ". End quote.

My answer:

Your claim that the AFC PASTORS are all in agreement. Sound good, but not true, not all AFC pastors are in agreement. I have emails record from some pastor, not in agreement with the situation. Of course being pastor licensed, most of AFC pastors are in fear, would not speak in front of the DS with obvious reason, under implied intimidation? In your email to me last year, 11/1/13 you said, in your letter, I quote,
"I understand your sentiments completely but the way we are organizationally structured, our AFC influence to the District decision making process has no teeth. It is in this regard that I have started talking with the

National Office to revisit the structure of Association as it relates to District leaders and come up with a better working relationship. The way it is set right now does not seem to be going anywhere. "End quote.

4, You claimed that, "It has become a stewardship issue wherein the assets has to be preserved to be used for Filipino ministry in the area. After all, Filipinos were the one who poured their heart and soul in the acquisition of this asset". End quote

My answer:

Your claim is broad, vague and superfluous, again not true! Here is the truth. The church property was paid in mortgage by the GCAC congregation for 28 years, from 1984 - 2012, your claim was exaggerated and have no bases. Therefore it may just a hearsay you heard.

5, You further claimed that "You also commend the SPD District under the leadership of Rev. Bill Malick for his diligence in executing his responsibilities as a leader."
End quote.

My answer:

With respect to Dr. Bill Malick, he mishandled the GCAC church situation, "NO CONGREGATIONAL MEETING AT ALL" he did call a GCAC congregational meeting by circular letter duly signed by him for 6/9/12, but later he RESCINDED in 6/7/12 during pastors informational meeting at Fullerton, CA. with you attending too, with many AFC pastors and some leaders members. The meeting was highly, emotionally, charge atmosphere between Pastor Fred. C and Dr. Malick including SPD AS Steve Riley. I raised my hand, given the permission to speak, I said, "the meeting shouting atmosphere was not glorifying to our God," I suggested to the body, to follow the standard procedure of appeal ". Note: AS Jay Letey was beside me.

6, You claim that "you have met with Rev. Bill Malick last week and he assured you that the money derived from the sale of the church building will be used for the growth and development of Filipino ministry in the Southern California area."

This is a current issue I will expound later in another email.

Here is God's Word! Revealed a very descriptive judgment words to "Irresponsible Shepherd ".

Using this Simile:
ISRAEL = C&MA, SPD,
SHEPHERD = DS Superintendent and AFC pastors,
FLOCK = GCAC Church,
SHEEP = GCAC MEMBERS.

Ezekiel 34:1-10 may very well apply eloquently, exactly to the C&MA and AFC. Must read and tremble at.

New King James Version (NKJV), IRRESPONSIBLE SHEPHERDS

1 And the word of the Lord came to me, saying, and 2 "Son of man, prophesy against the shepherds of Israel (C&MA, SPD, AFC) prophesy and say to them, 'Thus says the Lord God to the shepherds: "Woe to the shepherds of Israel who feed themselves! Should not the shepherds feed the flocks? 3 You eat the fat and clothe yourselves with the wool; you slaughter the fatlings, but you do not feed the flock. 4 The weak you have not strengthened, nor have you healed those who were sick, nor bound up the broken, nor brought back what was driven away, nor sought what was lost; but with force and cruelty you have ruled them. 5 So they were scattered because there was no shepherd; and they became food for all the beasts of the field when they were scattered. 6 My sheep wandered through all the mountains, and on every high hill; yes, My flock was scattered over the whole face of the earth, and no one was seeking or searching for them."

7 'Therefore, you shepherds, hear the word of the Lord: 8 "As I live," says the Lord God, "surely because My flock became a prey, and My flock became food for every beast of the field, because there was no shepherd, nor did My shepherds search for My flock, but the shepherds fed themselves and did not feed My flock"— 9 therefore, O shepherds, hear the word of the Lord! 10 Thus says the Lord God: "Behold, I am against the shepherds, and I will require my flock at their hand; I will cause them to cease feeding the sheep, and the shepherds shall feed themselves no more; for I will deliver my flock from their mouths, that they may no longer be food for them."...end

In summary, here is the truth, I am the witness.

1, The GCAC church was killed by the two " Constituted Authority " both conspired together in killing Jesus Christ Church by C&MA, SPD district and AFC LEADERSHIP,
2, Pastor Felix Ballon and You are part of the "Constituted Authority ".
3, AFC PASTORS are not all in agreement. Your claim is not true,

4, The church property was paid in mortgage by the GCAC congregation for 28 years.
5, Dr. Bill Malick, mishandled the GCAC church situation, "NO CONGREGATIONAL MEETING AT ALL
6, Sales $$$$ sharing? I will further reply later.

"Jesus body in GCAC church is dead." Ecclesiastical Euthanasia? The C&MA, National Office replied March 13, 2014. It was "final and binding".

In conclusion, the C&MA, SPD and AFC LEADERSHIP did ecclesiastical immorality and the Bible metaphors and God Words are very clear. The theological decisions are in a big question? IRRESPONSIBLE SHEPHERDS?

I grieve! Very truly,

Your brother in Christ.

Ven Cheock

Attachment F – Email to Our Brothers Mission with Thanks, March 14, 2014

From: Ven Cheock <vgcheock@yahoo.com>

Date: March 14, 2014 at 4:52:56 PM PDT
To: Lorenzo M Collado Jr <bongcollado@gmail.com>
Cc: Confidential
Subject: Re: Our brothers mission with thanks

Hi Pastor Bong, and greetings to all;

So nice to hear from you pastor, as brother in Christ. In due time, I will do diligence to share and expound later for I have a firsthand knowledge as former elder of GCAC. I think it's just fair that Alliance Churches should know the truth as accurate as possible.

Since I am a faithful Alliance church member for 35 years since 1978, believe in the Statement of Faith of C&MA, presently I have not departed the C&MA fold although grieving greatly since 2004, I am always in contact with AFC pastors for spiritual guidance and Alliance brothers and sisters in Christ.

Fortunately, I am not an Alliance Pastor, therefore, I have no C&MA license to lose or I am not answerable to any administrative superior other than our God Almighty, in Christ name only.

Therefore, thank you for getting in touch.
Jesus Christ be exalted!

Very heartfelt sincerely yours,

Brother Ven Cheock,
GCAC Remnant at large.

Attachment G – Email by Pastor Bong, March 14, 2014

On Mar 14, 2014, at 3:12 PM, "Lorenzo M Collado Jr"
<bongcollado@gmail.com> wrote:

Dear all,

Thank you for your continued interest in the Christian and Missionary
Alliance. As you know, I am an Official Licensed Worker of the Alliance and I
take pride and guard my license very zealously because of what it stands. I
also take pride in my association with the Alliance because of the very high
level of integrity that the leadership of the C&MA conduct their ministry in
pursuing the mission that God has for us as a denomination here in the U.S.
both at the District and National level. Having said that, I stand to put my
name on the line in the defense of this great denomination and its
leadership.

I need to respond to this email that our brother, Ven Cheock wrote in order
to set the record straight. In as much as there is in our bylaws the
"reversionary clause," we also have a stipulation on "constituted authority."
What this means is that we as pastors made a covenant during our licensing
interview as well as ordination interview to submit to the authority over us
which is the District Leadership and the National Leadership. And yearly, our
license is renewed on the condition that we are still in agreement to what
the Alliance is all about and implied in it is to continue to submit to the
constituted authority over us otherwise on our own accord, we need to
surrender our license back to the District if we have to act with integrity.

With this as a background, our pastor in GCAC, Fred Cheock was met by the
SPD District Leadership being represented by Rev. Bill Malick, the District
Superintendent with the concern that the church is in decline under his
pastoral leadership. Considering his age, he was offered a very generous
financial retirement package and frankly, the district is not obligated to do
that. Pastor Cheock refused the offer and instead he dug his heels and
rallied his church people to fight the District at all cost. They continued
meeting in the church facilities until finally, Pastor Cheock removed himself
from the church or so we thought.

The Association of Filipino Churches of the C&MA of which I am the president
was asked to intervene. I rallied the other pastors in the area and with one
voice, we supported the decision of the District to bring a change into the

church. We also met with you guys together with the leaders of the current occupants of the building led by Avery Schott, to explore different options in order to find a resolution to this conflict. Further, I appreciate the work of Ate Peth Manalac and Ate Nancy Ureta who boldly went to GCAC, attended their church services, try to talk them into submitting to the plan of revitalizing the GCAC with the old members going back and starting a fresh under the pastoral leadership of Pastor Felix Ballon, who in his generous heart and with the passion of seeing the church of Jesus Christ be just that, despite his busy church schedule of his own already. This plan was supported by the District Superintendent just so we will have a smooth transition. All of this effort failed because the current occupant of GCAC did not want to cooperate with the plan. They wanted it under their own terms and their lack of pastoral leadership is very troubling. So again this group has shown their disregard to constituted authority.

The most logical step therefore is to padlock the church by the District and the AFC pastors are all in agreement to this move. It has become a stewardship issue wherein the assets has to be preserved to be used for Filipino ministry in the area. After all, Filipinos were the one who poured their heart and soul in the acquisition of this asset. I also commend the SPD District under the leadership of Rev. Bill Malick for his diligence in executing his responsibilities as a leader.

I have met with Rev. Bill Malick last week and he assured me that the money derived from the sale of the church building will be used for the growth and development of Filipino ministry in the Southern California area. There are possible projects that we are looking into at this moment as a result of my meeting with the SPD pastors last week. Nothing is definite yet as we are still in the exploration stage. We invite your input also if you so desire. Be assured that this project is a collaboration between the District and AFC and I am looking forward to being a part of it with so much encouragement that the God of the universe is also our own personal God who will guide us in every step. After all it was His son Jesus who said that "...If I build my church, the gates of hell will not prevail against it." What a blessed hope we have in Jesus Christ. So let's work together for his soon return.

Pastor Bong Collado
AFC, President

Attachment H – Email: Our Brothers Mission with Thanks, March 13, 2014

From: Ven Cheock

From: Ven Cheock <vgcheock@yahoo.com>
Sent: Thursday, March 13, 2014 7:22 AM
Subject: Our Brothers Mission with Thanks

To all: my brothers and sisters in Christ.

I believe as we had concluded our efforts last Tuesday, 3/11/14, which Josh
will mail to us the C&MA reply.

Whatever actions and results in our GCAC restoration advocacy efforts was
worthy before the GCAC ministry for our Almighty God. While we perceive
differently, the next step of our individual mission assignment before God.
God will reward us accordingly.

As I said, looking beyond, who are our brothers? Or our neighbors? The
Good Samaritan parable that Jesus narrated is very vivid and clear. Some of
us can relax like the priest and the Levite and The Good Samaritan help!
Which of these three do you think became a neighbor to the man who fell
into the hands of the robbers?"
The answer was, "The one who showed mercy to him." So Jesus said to him,
"Go and do the same."

Our GCAC closure and suffering experience with C&MA, SPD LEADERSHIP is
not unique, we have witnessed the injustice schemes and results in many
brothers and sisters sufferings. Not only in our church, but also In St Louis,
Missouri, in New Jersey, in the Chinese church.

As I have slept and meditated for two nights, I am fully convinced, the other
churches need to be aware of this religious schemes of C&MA LEGAL
REVERSIONARY CLAUSE. Its original purpose is when church closes at the
request of the congregation.

But that was not the case, It was forced, padlocked the CHURCH, decided to
legally closed, then property sold, it was done on purpose by the C&MA, SPD

leadership to close the churches for the church assets and properties, in million of Dollars, in the guise or seeming appearance of furthering expansion ministry without regards to sufferings to hard won many souls to Jesus Christ.

I think I said enough, with heartfelt love for all.

My brotherly love,

Bro. Ven

Bible references:

Luke 10:29-37. The Good Samaritan

29 But the expert, wanting to justify himself, said to Jesus, "And who is my neighbor?
"30 Jesus replied, "A man was going down from Jerusalem to Jericho, and fell into the hands of robbers, who stripped him, beat him up, and went off, leaving him half dead.
31 Now by chance a priest was going down that road, but when he saw the injured man he passed by on the other side.
32 So too a Levite, when he came up to the place and saw him, passed by on the other side.
33 But a Samaritan who was traveling came to where the injured man was, and when he saw him, he felt compassion for him.
34 He went up to him and bandaged his wounds, pouring oil and wine on them. Then he put him on his own animal, brought him to an inn, and took care of him. 35 The next day he took out two silver coins and gave them to the innkeeper, saying, 'Take care of him, and whatever else you spend, I will repay you when I come back this way.'
36 Which of these three do you think became a neighbor to the man who fell into the hands of the robbers?"
37 The expert in religious law said, "The one who showed mercy to him." So Jesus said to him, "Go and do the same."

Attachment I – Final Appeal Letter to Dr. John Stumbo, November 8, 2013

Final Appeal Letter: to C&MA, national office. Complete copy. 11/8/13

To: Dr. John Stumbo, President CMA Board of Directors (via email) – CMA
8595 Explorer Drive Colorado Springs, CO 80920
Cc: South Pacific DEXCOM, Alliance of Filipino Churches (details below)
Date: November 8, 2013
Subject: Request to Cease and Desist on Sale of GCAC property and
Invalidation of Reversion

Gentlemen:

It has come to our attention that the property belonging to the Grace
Community Alliance Church in Baldwin Park has been and is currently under
escrow with a pending sale. This is alarming news as the events relating to
the reversion of property and dissolution of the congregation has been
clouded with contradicting promises from the district and questionable
transactions that we believe bordered on fraud and deception. This is
unconscionable and highly unbecoming of a supposedly prestigious
institution as the Christian and Missionary Alliance, to wit:

1. The District is entirely at fault for the current situation. The hiring of the
pastor without appropriate doctrinal and track record screening, as well as
the first and succeeding divisions of the church and subsequent reductions in
membership were due to the failures of the district in intervening and/or
replacing the pastor with all these issues in a timely and satisfactory
manner. It is definitely the district's fault for allowing the conflict to reach a
damage point which is now almost irreparable. Despite the district's
negligence and incompetence in handling the crisis, it has gone ahead to
punish the congregation who are actually THE victims of the district's
inadequate support and unpreparedness or incompetence in handling a crisis
situation.

2. The reversion of property to the district seems to have been handled
manipulatively, fraudulently and with the agenda of financial gain at the
expense of the congregation. The district manipulated the removal of Pastor
Hernan Pada as caretaker of GCAC in preparation for dissolution on grounds
that there is no available pastor for GCAC. The District subsequently

appointed the District Superintendent as Senior Pastor of GCAC with the agenda of declaring the board and congregation dissolved. This is a conflict of interest and the manipulation of events for financial gain.

3. GCAC has not been guilty of any of the 4 Property Reversion Events outlined in the Uniform Constitution and Bylaws of the CMA. There has been no disaffiliation. There has been no attempt not to abide by any of the purposes, usages, doctrines nor teachings of the CMA other than by the pastor himself whose tenure and existence is supposed to be under the district's oversight unless you consider the pastor's insubordination to be the congregation's insubordination which is totally unfair. There has been no obvious failure to be an accredited church and there has been no internal attempt to terminate the church's existence. Hence, there are no grounds for reversion other than arbitrariness, abuse of power and the desire for financial benefit.

4. It has also come to our attention that pastors of the Alliance of Filipino Churches were promised money from the proceeds of the sale of the GCAC property. Was it to silence their possible support for GCAC to avert the planned reversion of property? Even Pastor Hernan Pada was relieved of his custodial post last-minute to give way to the District Superintendent as Senior Pastor. Was this because Pastor Pada would refuse to dissolve GCAC and therefore prevent the desired reversion of property?

5. We noticed that there is a distinct similarity in the modus operandi of the SPD in the closure, dissolution and reversion of the property of our sister church at Paramount. Instead of providing a viable solution to either replace the last pastor and/or resolve the crisis in the congregation, the District sought instead to execute the path of least resistance for its obvious financial benefit. Instead of providing a Senior Pastor for the Paramount church or a possible merger with Pastor Steve Gusto of ABCD to make then avoid the burden of monthly rentals, the District has instead opted for the path of maximum financial gain where ABCD is paying rental for Paramount which is a fully paid church.

6. We also question if such unsupportive steps from the district to GCAC could be related to racial bias since GCAC is a church with a Filipino majority? The same is true with our sister church at Paramount. Had GCAC been a Caucasian church would the reversion have happened so quickly? We compare our case to the former Pasadena Alliance Church which the district had allowed to linger for so long with a congregation of less than a handful before finally reverting the property, we also suspect, to alleviate the

district's financial issues. This may have possible legal ramifications with both the State of California and the Federal Government itself.

7. We question if there are specific black-and-white procedures in the reversion of property back to the district and if there are any minutes or official notes or correspondence showing that the district had done due diligence to protect the interest of the flock and followed such specific steps in implementing the reversion process. The process has seemed to us as completely arbitrary and therefore an abuse of power instead of a demonstration of godly pastoral care.

8. Finally, we now realize that the previous promises of the district to restore GCAC has been deceptive and done in bad faith as there has never been any mention in writing that the property of GCAC would NOT revert to the district if the GCAC constituents would follow redemptive paths and a definite restorative process given the damage allowed by the District to transpire.

9. We are also aware of the District's attempts NOT to accept the amortization payments from the last batch of governing board members of GCAC to the point that that said board had to remit payments to an escrow account to avoid delinquency. It is now evident that the district, consistent with its current secular mindset and modus operandi, had no intentions of supporting nor ministering to the congregation but instead had this agenda all along to revert the property to the district for its financial benefits.

Gentlemen, the integrity of the CMA is at stake here. Are we really A.B. Simpson's vision of the Christian and MISSIONARY Alliance or have you deliberately deteriorated to become the Christian and MERCENARY Alliance? Are you sacrificially pastoral overseers for the flock of the Lord's church or is your sole interest that of financial gain considering the bankrupt history of the district ever since the administration of Don Brust? You do not need to be reminded that the economy of the church has always advanced with the confirmation of God's calling and not merely by the preservation of careers.

Each interest will have its own consequences coming from God Himself, or have we totally lost the fear of God in our dealings even within the church? Be reminded that our God who blesses is the same God who declared curses upon His own people and he is the same yesterday, today, and forever and is no respecter of persons. God gave us the choice to be blessed or be cursed. Whatever our choices be, may God dispense his consequences accordingly and quickly as He is faithful to His Word.

Have we even spent time in prayer and fasting to mourn these tragic failures as God's shepherds, prophets and priests or have we simply dealt with these issues as secular institution despots and administrators? God will be the judge.

We also appeal to you in the Lord's Name and for His sake to cease and desist from the sale of the GCAC property at least until any shadow of doubt has been cleared to the intelligent satisfaction of all. We will consider the cancellation or suspension of sale of the property as a redemptive gesture and an act of good faith on your part. Otherwise, we will be forced to use legal means to seek satisfaction and may even involve the press to make our case public and deter the district or any denomination for that matter from unbridled use of power to seek financial advantage at the expense of others.

The onus of proof that our suspicions are incorrect lies with the district. We anticipate a satisfactory response that covers even just the basic items we have presented above within ten (10) business days from the receipt of this registered mail, which includes:

1. Your response proving or disproving our contentions and suspicions to this notice and appeal, either by USPS mail or email
2. Any document denying or suspending the sale of the GCAC Baldwin Park property.

We are certain that these requests are reasonable; are hoping that we are dealing with reasonable people; and are praying that we ourselves will prove reasonable in this conversation.

Sincerely,

Grace Community Alliance Church Restoration Advocacy (non-profit)

End of references, by Ven Cheock

Attachment J – GCAC Brief History, April 16, 2014

Written by Ven Cheock

The writer was with GCAC for 26 years between 1978 and 2004. I left the Church in 2004. Currently I am not a member for any denomination. I consider myself a wandering GCAC member of this body of Christ.

GCAC Brief History:

In 1973, elder Fred Pamaran, a Filipino Alliance Christian from Mindanao, Philippines, with his compassion, formed a Filipino bible study group in Los Angeles. The number of members increased. Later, the group moved to Carmona/Washington Blvd area with Pastor A. Apelar as senior pastor. Together they officially formed the Grace Community Alliance Church (GCAC). GCAC Pastor H. Pada was the first Missionary to Orange County.

GCAC was affiliated as the first Filipino Alliance Church of the Christian and Missionary Alliance (USA). It was considered the "Mother Church" of the Filipino Alliance Churches in North America because other churches later spawned in Paramount, San Diego, San Francisco and as far as Seattle, Washington.

In 1978, the writer joined GCAC. At that time, there were three (3) clans making up the pillar of GCAC: the Pamaran/Antonio, Valdomar/David and Garcia families. In time, The Church congregation further increased in number. This is symbolic of Abraham, Isaac and Jacob, the 3 patriarchs of God's people.

Like any other churches, church leadership had its peaks and valleys. Church membership were affected, congregation joys and pains happened very much like the Jewish people in the bible.

In 2004, due to doctrinal and administrative issue of the new pastor, the church leadership was fragmented. This was reported to the Superintendent, but the situation was mishandled by the SPD district. 60-70 % of the congregation members left, wandering very much like the wandering Jews.

Currently, 40 years since its beginning, GCAC remnant members are around. On June 9, 2012, Sunday, I met with some brothers and sisters in the body of Christ of GCAC, including Pastor H. Pada, Jun Caro, Tony Unson, Pete

Quijano, Peth Manalac and others. Outside of GCAC, I also met some wandering GCAC Christian brothers and sisters, the Garcias, the Antonios and others. Previous wandering GCAC members were preparing to return, worship and fellowship with each other.

2012-2014, was the beginning of the end, Pastor Hernan Pada group was persuaded to move out by the C&MA Superintendent. Then irreconcilable issues ensued between the Superintendent and the current GCAC leaders. By June 10, 2012, the church property was forcibly padlocked by the C&MA South Pacific District (SPD) Superintendent, but reopened by the church leaders. No congregational meeting was ever called, pleads for GCAC restoration from previous GCAC members fell into deaf ears. Outside interventions also failed. Finally, the C&MA South Pacific District (SPD) Superintendent closed GCAC, dissolved the corporation, re padlocked the church and property was sold. These were all done without the consent of the congregation.